PICTURE THIS!
Shakespeare

William Shakespeare's

Romeo
and
Juliet

EDITED BY
Philip Page and Marilyn Pettit

ILLUSTRATED BY
Philip Page

BARRON'S

First edition for the United States, its territories and dependencies, the Philippine Republic, and Canada published in 2005 by Barron's Educational Series, Inc.

First published in Great Britain in 1999 by Hodder and Stoughton Limited
Copyright © 1999 Philip Page and Marilyn Pettit
Illustrations copyright © 1999 by Philip Page

All inquiries should be addressed to:
Barron's Educational Series, Inc.
250 Wireless Boulevard
Hauppauge, New York 11788
www.barronseduc.com

Library of Congress Catalog Card No.: 2004110790

ISBN-13: 978-0-7641-3144-8
ISBN-10: 0-7641-3144-3

Printed in China

9 8 7

Contents

About the play

Nearly everybody has heard of *Romeo and Juliet* ...
... and nearly everybody knows that it's a tragedy.

Not everybody knows that a tragedy has to follow rules, and end with a death.

Suicide, murder, or natural causes!
Not many die of natural causes in this play. The deaths are violent and horrible.

Read the play; be a detective and see if you can find the clues that tell you things are not going to end with the line: **"And they all lived happily ever after!"**

Once you've found the clues and noted them down, decide who *you* would put on trial for the murders, who *you* would blame for the suicides of the two young lovers!

Is this a love story, or a lesson about the stupidity of violence?

Cast of characters

Romeo Montague and Juliet Capulet
The star-crossed lovers.

Montague   Lady Montague
Romeo's worried father and loving mother.

Capulet   Lady Capulet
Juliet's selfish father and unhappy mother.

Mercutio
Romeo's friend, a joker who is quarrelsome.

Benvolio
Romeo's sensible friend.

Tybalt
Juliet's quarrelsome cousin.

Nurse
Juliet's nanny who helped bring her up.

Balthasar
Romeo's loyal servant.

Friar Laurence
A holy man who tries to help the young lovers.

Paris
A pleasant man who wants to marry Juliet.

Prince Escalus
Ruler of Verona who tries to keep order and fails.

Literary terms

alliteration The repetition of one or more beginning sounds, usually consonants, in a group of words.

comedy A form of literature in which characters are faced with moderate difficulties, but they overcome them and the story ends happily.

comic relief The use of a comic scene to interrupt intensely tragic or highly dramatic moments.

hyperbole Language that greatly overstates or exaggerates for rhetorical or comic effect.

irony Term indicating that the way something appears differs from reality, either in meaning, situation, or action. It is ironic when there is a difference between what is said and what is meant (verbal irony), what a character believes about a situation and what is reality, or what is intended by a character's actions and what is the actual outcome (dramatic irony).

metaphor A figure of speech that compares unlike objects without using connecting terms such as *like* or *as*.

oxymoron A statement that combines two terms usually seen as opposites. The effect created seems to be a contradiction, but is true. Some examples are *deafening silence, jumbo shrimp*.

personification A figure of speech in which objects or animals are given human qualities.

pun A play on words that have similar sounds but different meanings.

simile A figurative comparison using the words *like* or *as*. Some examples are *pretty as a picture, cunning like a fox*.

soliloquy A speech given in a drama, when characters speak their thoughts aloud while alone, thereby communicating their thoughts, mental state, intentions, and motives to the audience.

tragedy A form of literature in which the hero is destroyed by a character flaw and a set of forces that cause the hero considerable suffering. *Romeo & Juliet* is the ultimate tragedy. Romeo and Juliet are "star-crossed lovers." Fate says that Romeo and Juliet are not intended for each other. However, they make the mistake of believing that they can be together. This is their tragic flaw—they act too spontaneously without thinking through their actions.

Many examples of these terms have been pointed out for you throughout this book. Pay attention and you may find even more!

The Chorus is a person who comes onto the stage and tells the audience what is going to happen. Here he says that Romeo and Juliet's families do nothing but fight against each other. They only make peace when the two young lovers die.

Two households both alike in dignity
(In fair Verona, where we lay our scene)
From ancient grudge break to new mutiny,
Where civil blood makes civil hands unclean.
From forth the fatal loins of these two foes
A pair of star-crossed lovers take their life,
Whose misadventured piteous overthrows
Doth with their death bury their parents' strife.
The fearful passage of their death-marked love
And the continuance of their parents' rage,
Which, but their children's end, nought could remove,
Is now the two hours' **traffic** of our stage;
The which, if you with patient ears attend,
What here shall miss, our toil shall strive to mend.

Think about it
Why does the Chorus tell the whole story?
Do you think that has ruined the story for us?
Why does he tell us that the play will only last two hours?
(Think about Shakespeare's theater and where the audience might be.)

traffic – business

A fight breaks out between the servants of the Montague family and the Capulet family. Benvolio (a Montague) and Tybalt (a Capulet) arrive.

The quarrel is between our masters and us their men.

Here comes of the house of the Montagues.

Quarrel, I will back thee.

Do you **bite your thumb** at us, sir?

I do bite my thumb, sir.

Do you quarrel, sir?

Quarrel, sir? No sir.

But if you do, sir, I am for you.

Part fools, put up your swords, you know not what you do.

Turn thee, Benvolio, look upon thy death.

bite your thumb – an insulting gesture

2

I do but keep the peace.

What, drawn, and talk of peace?

I hate the word, as I hate hell, all Montagues, and thee.

The people of Verona, fed up with the two families fighting, attack the Montagues and Capulets.

Down with the Capulets!

Down with the Montagues!

Even old Capulet and old Montague rush to join in!

Give me my long sword, ho!

Hold me not. Let me go!

A crutch, a crutch! Why call you for a sword?

Thou shalt not stir one foot to seek a foe.

<table>
<tr><td>

**Act 1
Scene 1**

</td><td>

The Prince arrives and says that if ever there is fighting again, Capulet and Montague will be punished by death. Montague, Lady Montague, and Benvolio talk about Romeo's strange moods.

</td><td>

</td></tr>
</table>

Prince: Rebellious subjects, enemies to peace,
Profaners of this neighbor-stained steel –
Will they not hear? What ho! You men, you beasts!
That quench the fire of your pernicious rage
With **purple fountains** issuing from your veins,
On pain of torture from those bloody hands
Throw your mistempered weapons to the ground
And hear the sentence of your moved prince.
Three civil brawls bred of an airy word
By thee, old Capulet, and Montague,
Have thrice disturbed the quiet of our streets.
If ever you disturb our streets again
Your lives shall pay the **forfeit of the peace**.
For this time all the rest depart away.
You, Capulet, shall go along with me,
And Montague, come you this afternoon,
To know our farther pleasure in this case.
Once more, on pain of death, all men depart.

purple fountains – blood

forfeit – penalty for breaching the peace

[*Everybody leaves except Montague,
Lady Montague, and Benvolio*]

Lady Montague: O where is Romeo? Saw you him today?
Right glad I am he was not at this fray.

Benvolio: Madam, an hour before the worshipped sun
Peered forth the golden window of the east,
A troubled mind drove me to walk abroad,
Where underneath the grove of sycamore
That westward rooteth from this city side
So early walking did I see your son.
Towards him I made, but he was 'ware of me
And stole into the covert of the wood.

Literary terms

"Peered forth the golden window" is an example of *personification*.

4

Montague: Many a morning hath he there been seen,
With tears augmenting the fresh morning's dew,
Adding to clouds more clouds with his deep sighs.
Away from light steals home my heavy son
And private in his chamber pens himself,
Shuts up his windows, locks fair daylight out
And makes himself an artificial night.

Benvolio: My noble uncle, do you know the cause?

Montague: I neither know it nor can learn of him.

Benvolio: Have you **importuned him** by any means?

Montague: Both by myself and many other friends.
Could we but learn from whence his sorrows grow,
We would as willingly give cure as know.

[*Enter Romeo*]

Benvolio: See where he comes. So please you step aside;
I'll know his grievance or be much denied.

> **Literary terms**
>
> "Adding to clouds more clouds" is an example of *hyperbole.*

Romeo locks himself in his room and his father is worried.

importuned him – asked him

> **Think about it**
>
> What do you think is bothering Romeo?
>
> Why is he getting up early and then later shutting himself in his room?
>
> What kind of friend is Benvolio?

Benvolio finds out that Romeo is in love but the girl does not love him. He tries to persuade Romeo that there are plenty of other girls he can date.

What sadness lengthens Romeo's hours?

Not having that, which, having, makes them short.

In love?

Out.

Tell me in sadness who is it that you love?

In sadness, cousin, I do love a woman.

I aimed so near when I supposed you loved.

Then she hath sworn that she will still live chaste?

She hath.

Forget to think of her. Examine other beauties.

Thou canst not teach me to forget.

| Act 1 Scene 2 | Paris wants to marry Juliet. Her father is not sure about this. He suggests that Paris come to the party he is having that night. He sends a servant off with the list of guests to invite. |

What say you to my suit?

My child is yet a stranger in the world, she hath not seen the change of fourteen years.

But woo her, gentle Paris, and get her heart.

This night I hold an old accustomed feast. One more, most welcome, makes my number more.

Go, find those persons out whose names are written there, and to them say, my house and welcome on their pleasure stay.

The servant cannot read but he meets Romeo and Benvolio in the street and asks them to help him.

Can you read?

Ay, if I know the letters and the language.

Whither should they come?

To our house. My master is the great rich Capulet.

If you be not of the house of Montague I pray come and **crush** a cup of wine.

At this same ancient feast sups the fair Rosaline, whom thou so loves.

Go thither and with **unattainted** eye compare her face with some that I shall show and I will make thee think thy swan a crow.

One fairer than my love! The all-seeing sun ne'er saw her match since first the world begun.

Tut, you saw her fair, none else being by.

I'll go along, no such sight to be shown, But to rejoice in splendor of mine own.

crush – drink

unattainted – unbiased, unprejudiced

8

<table>
<tr><td>**Act 1
Scene 3**</td><td>Juliet's mother asks her to take a
good look at Paris at the party that
night, because she might have to
marry him.</td></tr>
</table>

Lady Capulet: Thou knowest my daughter's of a pretty age.

Nurse: Faith, I can tell her age unto an hour.

Lady Capulet: She's not fourteen.

Nurse: I'll lay fourteen of my teeth
(and yet, to my **teen** be it spoken, I have but four)
She's not fourteen. How long is it now
To **Lammas-tide**?

teen: sorrow

Lammas-tide: August 1st

Lady Capulet: A fortnight and odd days.

Nurse: Even or odd, of all days in the year,
Come Lammas Eve at night shall she be fourteen.
Thou wast the prettiest babe that e'er I nursed.
And I might live to see thee married once,
I have my wish.

Lady Capulet: Marry, that "marry" is the very theme
I came to talk of. Tell me, daughter Juliet,
How stands your dispositions to be married?

Juliet: It is an honor that I dream not of.

Nurse: An honor. Were not I thine only nurse
I would say thou hadst sucked wisdom from thy teat.

Lady Capulet: Well, think of marriage now. Younger than you
Here in Verona, ladies of esteem,
Are made already mothers. By my count
I was your mother much upon these years
That you are now a maid. Thus then in brief:
The valiant Paris seeks you for his love.

Nurse: A man, young lady! Lady, such a man
As all the world – why, he's **a man of wax**.

a man of wax – a perfect man

Lady Capulet: Verona's summer hath not such a flower.

Nurse: Nay, he's a flower, in faith a very flower.

Lady Capulet: What say you? Can you love the gentleman?
This night you shall behold him at our feast;
Read o'er the volume of young Paris' face
And find delight writ there with beauty's pen.
Speak briefly, can you like of Paris' love?

Juliet must look at him closely, like reading a book.

Juliet: I'll look to like, if looking liking move,
But no more deep will I endart mine eye
Than your consent gives strength to make it fly.

Think about it

Do you think Juliet is too young to get married?

She says that she will listen to her parents' advice. How do we know that she won't?

Literary terms

"beauty's pen" is a good example of *personification*.

The Montagues are on their way to the Capulets' party. Romeo is worried about what might happen there.

'**Tis no wit** to go. I dreamt a dream tonight.

And so did I.

Well what was yours?

That dreamers often lie.

In bed asleep, while they do dream things true.

O then I see Queen Mab hath been with you.

Queen Mab! What's she?

She is the fairies' midwife.

Peace, Mercutio, thou talk'st of nothing.

True, I talk of dreams which are the children of an idle brain.

Supper is done and we shall come too late.

I fear too early, for **my mind misgives**
Some consequence yet hanging in the stars
Shall bitterly begin his fearful date
With this night's revels.

'**Tis no wit** – it's not wise
my mind misgives – I'm worried

Literary terms
The play on the two meanings of the word lie (a falsehood or prone position) is a good example of a *pun*.

Romeo: What lady is that which doth enrich the hand
Of yonder knight?

Servingman: I know not, sir.

Romeo: O! she doth teach the torches to burn bright!
It seems she hangs upon the cheek of night
Like a rich jewel in an Ethiop's ear —
Beauty too rich for use, for earth too dear!
So shows a snowy dove trooping with crows,
As yonder lady o'er her fellows shows.
Did my heart love till now? Forswear it, sight!
For I ne'er saw true beauty till this night.

Romeo notices how beautiful Juliet is.

Tybalt: This by his voice should be a Montague.
Fetch me my **rapier**, boy. What! dares the slave
Come hither, cover'd with an **antic face**,
To fleer and scorn at our solemnity?
Now by the stock and honor of my kin,
To strike him dead I hold it not a sin.

rapier – sword
antic face – mask

Capulet: Why, how now, kinsman! Wherefore storm
you so?

Tybalt: Uncle, this is a Montague, our foe.

Capulet: Young Romeo, is it?
Content thee, gentle coz, let him alone:
He bears him like **a portly gentleman**;
And, to say truth, Verona brags of him
To be a virtuous and well-governed youth.
I would not for the wealth of all this town
Here in my house do him disparagement;
Therefore be patient, take no note of him:
It is my will.

Literary terms

"Like a rich jewel" and "like a portly gentleman" are good examples of *simile*.

a portly gentleman – a well-mannered person

Tybalt: I'll not endure him!

Capulet: He shall be endured:
What! I say, he shall. Go to.
Am I the master here or you?
You'll not endure him!
You'll make a mutiny among my guests!

Tybalt: I will withdraw, but this intrusion shall,
Now seeming sweet, convert to bitter gall. [*Tybalt leaves*]

Romeo: [*to Juliet*] If I profane with my unworthiest hand
This holy shrine, the gentle sin is this:
My lips, two blushing pilgrims, ready stand
To smooth that rough touch with a tender kiss.

Juliet: Good pilgrim, you do wrong your hand too much,
Which mannerly devotion shows in this;
For saints have hands that pilgrims' hands do touch,
And palm to palm is holy **palmers**' kiss.

Romeo: Have not saints lips, and holy palmers too?

Juliet: Ay, pilgrim, lips that they must use in prayer.

Romeo: O! then, dear saint, let lips do what hands do;
They pray, grant thou, lest faith turn to despair.

Juliet: Saints do not move, though grant for prayers' sake.

Romeo: Then move not, while my prayer's effect I take.
Thus from my lips, by thine, my sin is purged. [*Kissing her*]

Juliet: Then have my lips the sin that they have took.

Romeo: Sin from my lips? O trespass sweetly urged!
Give me my sin again.

Literary terms

"My lips, two blushing pilgrims" is a good example of a *metaphor*.

palmer – pilgrim

Think about it

Romeo went to see Rosaline and now he's fallen in love with Juliet! What do you think of him now?

What do you think of his "pick up" lines to Juliet?

What adjectives would you use to describe Tybalt?

Can you guess what might happen between Tybalt and Romeo?

Madam, your mother craves a word with you.

What is her mother?

Her mother is the lady of the house. I nursed her daughter that you talked withal.

I tell you, he that can lay hold of her shall have the **chinks**.

Is she a Capulet? O dear account. **My life is my foe's debt**.

Away, begone.

What's he that now is going out of door? Go ask his name.

If he be married, my grave is like to be my wedding bed.

His name is Romeo, and a Montague, the only son of your great enemy.

My only love sprung from my only hate.
Too early seen unknown, and known too late.
Prodigious birth of love it is to me
That I must love a loathèd enemy.

chinks – money   **prodigious** – unlucky
My life is my foe's debt – My happiness is
   in the hands of my enemy

Literary terms

"my grave is like to be my wedding bed" is a good example of *hyperbole*.

Act 2 Scene 2	Romeo wants to be alone and has climbed over a wall into a garden to escape from his friends. He sees and hears Juliet on a balcony. They tell each other that they are in love. They also know this will bring trouble.

Romeo: But, soft! What light through yonder window breaks?
It is the East, and Juliet is the sun!
It is my lady; O! it is my love:
O! that she knew she were.
She speaks, yet she says nothing. What of that?
I am too bold. 'Tis not to me she speaks.
See! how she leans her cheek upon her hand:
O! that I were a glove upon that hand,
That I might touch that cheek.

Juliet: Ay me!

Romeo: O! speak again, **bright angel; for thou art
As glorious to this night, being o'er my head,
As is a winged messenger of heaven.**

Juliet: O Romeo, Romeo! **Wherefore art thou Romeo**?
Deny thy father, and refuse thy name;
Or, if thou wilt not, be but sworn my love,
And I'll no longer be a Capulet.
'Tis but thy name that is my enemy;
What's Montague? It is nor hand, nor foot,
Nor arm, nor face, nor any other part
Belonging to a man. O! be some other name!
What's in a name? That which we call a rose
By any other word would smell as sweet.

Romeo: I take thee at thy word.
Call me but love, and I'll be new baptized.
Henceforth I never will be Romeo.

**Juliet: What man art thou, that, thus bescreened in night,
So stumblest on my counsel?**

Literary terms

Romeo's speech beginning "But, soft!" and Juliet's speech beginning "O Romeo, Romeo!" are both good examples of a *soliloquy*.

Juliet seems like an angel to Romeo.

Juliet asks why he has to be called Romeo.

Literary terms

"That which we call a rose by any other word would smell as sweet" is a good example of a *metaphor*.

Juliet asks who is there, hidden by the dark night, who is overhearing her.

Romeo: I know not how to tell thee who I am.
My name, dear saint, is hateful to myself,
Because it is an enemy to thee.

Juliet: Art thou not Romeo, and a Montague?
How camest thou hither, tell me, and wherefore?
The orchard walls are high and hard to climb,
And the place death, considering who thou art,
If any of my kinsmen find thee here.

Romeo: I have night's cloak to hide me from their eyes;

Juliet: Thou knowest the mask of night is on my face,
Else would a maiden blush bepaint my cheek
For that which thou hast heard me speak tonight.
Dost thou love me? I know thou wilt say, "Ay;"
If thou dost love, pronounce it faithfully:
**Or if thou thinkest I am too quickly won,
I'll frown and be perverse and say thee nay**,
So thou wilt woo; but else, not for the world.

Romeo: Lady, by yonder blessed moon I vow.

Juliet: O! swear not by the moon, the inconstant moon,
That monthly changes in her circled orb
Lest that thy love prove likewise variable.
Do not swear at all;
Or, if thou wilt, swear by thy gracious self
And I'll believe thee.
**Although I joy in thee,
I have no joy of this contract tonight.
It is too rash, too unadvised, too sudden.**

Romeo: O! wilt thou leave me so unsatisfied?

Juliet: What satisfaction canst thou have tonight?

Romeo: The exchange of thy love's faithful vow for mine.

Juliet: I gave thee mine before thou didst request it.

[*The Nurse calls*]

I hear some noise within. Dear love, adieu.
Stay but a little, I will come again.

Literary terms

"night's cloak" and "mask of night" are good examples of *personification*.

Juliet wonders if Romeo thinks she's too eager.

Juliet is worried that things seem to be happening too quickly.

anon – in a moment   **my ghostly friar's close cell** – Friar Laurence's room

<table>
<tr><td>

**Act 2
Scene 3**

</td><td>

Friar Laurence is collecting herbs to make medicines. Romeo arrives and tells him about his love for Juliet and how he wants to be married to her.

</td></tr>
</table>

Friar Laurence: Now, ere the sun advance his burning eye
The day to cheer and night's dank dew to dry,
I must upfill this **osier cage** of ours
With baleful weeds and precious-juicèd flowers.
Within the infant rind of this weak flower
Poison hath residence and medicine power:
For this, being smelt, with that part cheers each part;
Being tasted, slays all senses with the heart.

Romeo: Good morrow, father!

Friar Laurence: What early tongue so sweet saluteth me?
Young son, it argues a distempered head
So soon to bid good morrow to thy bed.
Therefore thy earliness doth me assure
Thou art uproused with some distemperature;
Or if not so, then here I hit it right:
Our Romeo hath not been in bed tonight.

Romeo: That last is true. The sweeter rest was mine.

Friar Laurence: God pardon sin! Wast thou with Rosaline?

Romeo: With Rosaline, my ghostly father? No.
I have forgot that name, and that name's woe.

Friar Laurence: That's my good son. But where hast thou been, then?

Romeo: I'll tell thee, ere thou ask it me again.
I have been feasting with mine enemy,
Where on a sudden one hath wounded me,
That's by me wounded.

Friar Laurence: Be plain, good son, and homely in thy drift.

osier cage – willow basket

Literary terms

"his burning eye" is a good example of *personification*.

Friar Laurence knows that Romeo has something on his mind because he is up so early.

Romeo: Then plainly know my heart's dear love is set
On the fair daughter of rich Capulet.
As mine on hers, so hers is set on mine,
And all combined, save what thou must combine
By holy marriage; but this I pray,
That thou consent to marry us today.

Friar Laurence: Holy Saint Francis, what a change is here!
Is Rosaline, whom thou didst love so dear,
So soon forsaken? Young men's love then lies
Not truly in their hearts, but in their eyes.
And art thou changed? pronounce this sentence then:
Women may fall, when there's no strength in men.

Friar Laurence is shocked. First Rosaline; now Juliet. He thinks that Romeo must fall in love with the way a girl looks and not with what she is like.

Romeo: Thou chid'st me oft for loving Rosaline.

Friar Laurence: For doting, not for loving, pupil mine.

Romeo: And bad'st me bury love.

Friar Laurence: Not in a grave,
To lay one in, another out to have.

Romeo: I pray thee, chide me not. Her I love now
Doth grace for grace and love for love allow.
The other did not so.

Friar Laurence: O! she knew well
Thy love did read by rote that could not spell.
But come, young waverer, come, go with me,
In one respect I'll thy assistant be;
For this alliance may so happy prove,
To turn your households' rancour to pure love.

He thinks that Rosaline knew Romeo wasn't properly in love with her.

Romeo: O! let us hence: I stand on sudden haste.

Friar Laurence: Wisely and slow; they stumble that run fast.

Think about it

We know that the lovers die. We know that Friar Laurence is collecting herbs that can make a person seem dead. Can you guess what might happen to one of these lovers?

Why does Friar Laurence agree to marry Romeo and Juliet? Do you agree with him?

| **Act 2 Scene 4** | It is the morning after the Capulets' party. Mercutio and Benvolio are waiting for Romeo. Mercutio is worried that Romeo might have to fight Tybalt. |

Where the devil should this Romeo be? Came he not home tonight?

Not to his father's.

That Rosaline torments him so that he will sure run mad.

Tybalt hath sent a letter to his father's house.

A challenge on my life.

Romeo will answer it.

And is he a man to encounter Tybalt?

Why, what is Tybalt?

More than Prince of Cats. A duelist, a very good blade.

Here comes Romeo.

The Nurse arrives, looking for Romeo. Mercutio and Benvolio tease her.

Here's goodly gear.

My fan, Peter.

Good Peter, to hide her face, for her fan's the fairer face.

God ye good **morrow**, gentlemen.

God ye good **e'en** fair gentlewoman.

Is it good e'en?

'Tis no less, for the bawdy hand of the dial is now upon the prick of noon.

What a man are you?

Where may I find the young Romeo?

I am the youngest of that name.

If you be he sir, I desire some confidence with you.

She will **indite** him to some supper.

A bawd! A bawd!

Romeo, will you come to your father's? We'll to dinner thither.

I will follow you.

morrow – morning   **e'en** – afternoon   **indite** – invite

Literary terms

This scene is a good example of *comic relief*.

21

| **Act 2 Scene 4** | Romeo and the Nurse make plans for the wedding. His servant will give her a rope ladder so that Romeo can climb up to Juliet's room after the wedding. The Nurse also tells Romeo about Paris liking Juliet! | |

Nurse: Pray you, sir, a word. And as I told you, my young Lady bid me inquire you out. What she bid me say I will keep to myself. But first let me tell ye, if ye should lead her in a fool's paradise, as they say, it were a very gross kind of behavior.

Romeo: Nurse, commend me to thy lady and mistress. Bid her devise some means to come to **shrift** this afternoon. And there she shall at Friar Laurence' cell, Be shrived and married.

shrift – confession

Nurse: This afternoon, sir? Well, she shall be there.

Romeo: And stay, good nurse, behind the abbey wall. Within this hour my man shall be with thee And bring thee **cords made like a tackled stair**, Which to the high **topgallant** of my joy Must be my convoy in the secret night.

a rope ladder
topgallant – highest mast of a ship

Nurse: Now, God in heaven bless thee! O! there's a nobleman in town, one Paris, that would fain lay knife aboard; but she, good soul, **had as lief** see a toad, a very toad, as see him.

had as lief – would rather

Romeo: Commend me to thy lady.

Nurse: Ay, a thousand times.

Think about it

What do you think about the Nurse from this scene?

Why is it important to remind us about Paris?

<table>
<tr><td>**Act 2
Scene 5**</td><td>Juliet waits impatiently for the Nurse.</td></tr>
</table>

The clock struck nine when I did send the Nurse.

In half an hour she promised to return.

Perchance she cannot meet him.

Now is the sun upon the highmost hill of this day's journey . . .

. . . and from nine till twelve is three long hours, yet she is not come.

O God she comes.

O honey Nurse, what news?

I am aweary. Fie, how my bones ache.

I would thou hadst my bones and I thy news.

Act 2 Scene 5	The Nurse returns to tell Juliet the wedding plans. At first she teases Juliet by not telling her what she wants to know.	

Juliet: Nay, come, I pray thee, speak.
Good, good nurse, speak.

Nurse: Jesu! What haste? Can you not stay awhile?
Do you not see that I am out of breath?

Juliet: How art thou out of breath when thou haste breath
To say to me that thou art out of breath?
The excuse that thou dost make in this delay
Is longer than the tale thou dost excuse.
Is thy news good, or bad? Answer to that.
Say either, and I'll **stay the circumstance**.   wait for the details
Let me be satisfied; is't good or bad?

Nurse: Well, you have made a simple choice. You know not
how to choose a man. Romeo? No, not he. Though his face be
better than any man's, yet his leg excels all men's, and for a
hand, and a foot, and a body, though they are not to be talked
on, yet they are past compare. He is not the flower of courtesy,
but, I'll warrant him, as gentle as a lamb. Go thy ways, wench.
Serve God. What, have you dined at home?

Juliet: No, no. But all this did I know before.
What says he of our marriage? What of that?

Nurse: Lord, how my head aches! What a head have I!
It beats as it would fall in twenty pieces.
My back o' t'other side! Ah, my back, my back!
Beshrew your heart for sending me about
To catch my breath with **jaunting up and down**.   trudging about

Juliet: I' faith, I am sorry that thou art not well.
Sweet, sweet, sweet nurse, tell me, what says my love?

24

Nurse: Your love says, like an honest gentleman, and a courteous, and a kind, and a handsome, and, I warrant, a virtuous, – Where is your mother?

Juliet: Where is my mother? Why, she is within. Where should she be? How oddly thou repliest: "Your love says, like an honest gentleman, Where is your mother?"

Nurse: O! God's lady dear, are you so hot? Is this the **poultice** for my aching bones? Henceforward do your messages yourself.

poultice – medical dressing

Juliet: Here's such a **coil**. Come, what says Romeo?

coil – fuss

Nurse: Have you got leave to go to **shrift** today?

shrift – confession

Juliet: I have.

Nurse: Then hie you hence to Friar Laurence' cell. There stays a husband to make you a wife. **Now comes the wanton blood up in your cheeks**; **They'll be in scarlet straight at any news**. Hie you to church. I must another way, To fetch a ladder, by the which your love Must climb a **bird's nest** soon when it is dark; I am the drudge and toil in your delight, But you shall bear the burden soon at night. Go. I'll to dinner. Hie you to the cell.

Juliet is blushing with excitement.

Juliet's bedroom

Juliet: Hie to high fortune! Honest nurse, farewell.

Literary terms

The play on the meanings of the words "hie" and "high" is a good example of a *pun*.

Think about it

What words does the Nurse say to make Juliet impatient?

Why do you think the Nurse teases Juliet?

What type of relationship do they have?

| Act 2 Scene 6 | Juliet arrives at Friar Laurence's cell to get married to Romeo. |

So smile the heavens upon this holy act, that after hours with sorrow chide us not.

Amen! But come what sorrow can, it cannot **countervail** the exchange of joy that one short minute gives me in her sight.

It is enough I may but call her mine.

These violent delights have violent ends.

Here comes the lady.

Ah! Juliet.

My true love is grown to such excess I cannot **sum up sum** of half my wealth.

countervail – equal

Literary terms

"violent delights" is a good example of an *oxymoron*.

Come, come with me and we will make short work; For, by your leaves, you shall not stay alone Till Holy Church incorporates two in one.

sum up sum – count the total

Act 3 Scene 1	The day is hot, and on the streets of Verona the youths are ready for trouble.

I pray thee, good Mercutio, let's retire: the day is hot, the Capulets abroad, and, if we meet, we shall not 'scape a brawl.

Come, thou art as hot in thy mood as any in Italy.

Thou wilt quarrel with a man for cracking nuts because thou hast hazel eyes!

Here come the Capulets.

I care not.

A word with one of you.

And but one word with one of us? Couple it with something, make it a word and a blow.

Mercutio, thou consortest with Romeo . . .

Consort! What, dost thou make us minstrels?

Here's my fiddlestick; here's that shall make you dance.

Literary terms

"A word with one of you" is a good example of *alliteration*.

27

We talk here in the public haunt of men. Here all eyes gaze on us.

Let them gaze; I will not budge for no man's pleasure, I.

Well, peace be with you, sir. Here comes my man.

Romeo ... thou art a villain.

Tybalt, the reason that I have to love thee doth much excuse such a greeting.

Villain am I none, therefore farewell; I see thou knowest me not.

<table>
<tr><td>

**Act 3
Scene 1**

</td><td>

Tybalt and Mercutio fight. Romeo tries to stop them but Tybalt wounds Mercutio, who later dies. Tybalt comes back after Romeo. They fight and Romeo kills Tybalt. Now he has to run away.

</td><td>

</td></tr>
</table>

Tybalt: Boy, this shall not excuse the injuries
That thou hast done me. Therefore turn and draw.

Romeo: I do protest I never injured thee,
But love thee better than thou canst devise,
Till thou shalt know the reason of my love.
And so, good Capulet, which name I tender
As dearly as mine own, be satisfied.

Romeo has to like Tybalt now because he has married Juliet, who is Tybalt's cousin. He can't tell him yet, though. This is dramatic irony.

Mercutio: O calm, dishonorable, vile submission!
            [*Mercutio draws his sword*]
Tybalt, you ratcatcher, will you walk?

Tybalt: What wouldst thou have with me?

Mercutio gets Tybalt to fight because he thinks he should defend Romeo's honor.

Mercutio: Good King of Cats, nothing but one of your nine lives, that I mean to make bold withal, and, as you shall use me hereafter, **dry-beat** the rest of the eight.
            [*Tybalt draws his sword*]

dry-beat – thrash without drawing blood

Tybalt: I am for you.
            [*Tybalt and Mercutio fight*]

Romeo: Gentle Mercutio, put thy rapier up.
Gentlemen, for shame, forbear this outrage!
Tybalt, Mercutio! The Prince expressly hath
Forbidden this **bandying** in Verona streets.
Hold, Tybalt! Good Mercutio!
            [*Tybalt and the Capulets leave*]

Literary terms

"ratcatcher" is a good example of a *metaphor*.

---

bandying – fighting

Mercutio: I am hurt. A plague o' both your houses! I am sped.
Is he gone, and hath nothing?

Benvolio: What! art thou hurt?

Mercutio: Ay, ay, a scratch, a scratch. Marry, 'tis enough.
Ask for me tomorrow and you shall find me a grave man.
Why the devil came you between us? I was hurt under your arm.

Literary terms

The play on the meanings of the word "grave" (burial site or serious) is a good example of a *pun*.

Romeo: I thought all for the best.

Mercutio: Help me into some house, Benvolio,
Or I shall faint. A plague o' both your houses!
They have made worms' meat of me.

Romeo: This gentleman, the Prince's near ally,
My very friend, hath got his mortal hurt
In my behalf. My reputation stained
With Tybalt's slander – Tybalt, that an hour
Hath been my cousin! O sweet Juliet,
Thy beauty hath made me effeminate,
And in my temper softened valor's steel!

Benvolio: O Romeo, Romeo, brave Mercutio's dead.

Romeo: This day's black fate on more days doth depend.
This but begins the woe others must end.

Benvolio: Here comes the furious Tybalt back again.

Romeo: Alive! in triumph, and Mercutio slain!
Now, Tybalt, take the "villain" back again
That late thou gavest me, for Mercutio's soul
Is but a little way above our heads,
Staying for thine to keep him company.
Either thou, or I, or both, must go with him.

Tybalt: Thou wretched boy, that didst consort him here,
Shall with him hence.
              [*Romeo and Tybalt fight. Tybalt is killed*]

Benvolio: Romeo, away, be gone!
The prince will doom thee death if thou art taken.

Romeo: O! I am Fortune's fool.

Literary terms

"worms' meat" is a good example of a *metaphor*.

Think about it

What do you think of Romeo's behavior in this scene?

Do you feel sorry for Mercutio?

Do you feel sorry for Tybalt?

| **Act 3 Scene 1** | The Prince arrives and Benvolio explains what happened. Lady Capulet wants the Prince to execute Romeo, but he banishes him instead. |

Benvolio, who began this bloody fray?

Tybalt, here slain, whom Romeo's hand did slay.

Tybalt, deaf to peace, tilts with piercing steel at Mercutio's breast.

Romeo cries aloud, "Friends, part!" Tybalt hit the life of stout Mercutio and fled.

But by and by comes back to Romeo and they go like lightning.

Ere I could draw to part them, was Tybalt slain.

He is kinsman to the Montague, he speaks not true.

I beg for justice, which thou, Prince, must give. Romeo slew Tybalt, Romeo must not live.

Romeo slew him, he slew Mercutio. Who now the price of his dear blood doth owe?

Immediately we do exile him hence. Else, when he is found, that hour is his last.

<table>
<tr><td>

**Act 3
Scene 2**

</td><td>

The Nurse returns but she can't speak properly. She is so upset. Juliet works out finally that Romeo has killed Tybalt and that he has been banished from Verona.

</td><td></td></tr>
</table>

Juliet: Now nurse, what news? What hast thou there?
The cords that Romeo bade thee fetch?

the cords – the rope ladder

Nurse: Ay, ay, the cords.   [*She throws them down*]

Juliet: What news? Why dost thou wring thy hands?

Nurse: Ah **weraday**, he's dead, he's dead, he's dead!
We are undone, lady, we are undone!
Alack the day, he's gone, he's killed, he's dead!

weraday – an expression of sorrow

Juliet: Can heaven be so envious?

Nurse: Romeo can.
Though heaven cannot. O! Romeo, Romeo,
Who ever would have thought it? Romeo!

Juliet: What devil art thou that dost torment me thus?
This torture should be roared in dismal hell.
Hath Romeo slain himself? Say thou but "Ay,"
And that bare vowel "I" shall poison more
Than the death-darting eye of **cockatrice**.

Juliet is trying to get sense out of the Nurse.

cockatrice – a mythical animal that could kill just by looking at its victim

Nurse: I saw the wound. I saw it with mine eyes,
(God save the mark!) here on his manly breast –
A piteous **corse**, a bloody piteous corse,
Pale, pale as ashes, all bedaubed in blood,
All in gore blood. I **swoonèd** at the sight.

corse – corpse

swoonèd – fainted

Juliet: O break, my heart, poor bankrupt, break at once!
To prison, eyes; ne'er look on liberty.
Vile earth to earth resign; end motion here,
And thou and Romeo press one heavy bier.

Nurse: O Tybalt, Tybalt, the best friend I had!
O courteous Tybalt, honest gentleman,
That ever I should live to see thee dead!

Juliet: What storm is this that blows so contrary?
Is Romeo slaughtered and is Tybalt dead?
My dearest cousin, and my dearer lord?
Then, dreadful trumpet, sound the general doom!
For who is living if those two are gone?

Nurse: Tybalt is gone, and Romeo banished;
Romeo, that killed him – he is banished.

Juliet: O God, did Romeo's hand shed Tybalt's blood?

Nurse: It did, it did, alas the day! it did.

Juliet: O serpent heart, hid with a flow'ring face!
Did ever dragon keep so fair a cave?
Beautiful tyrant, fiend angelical!
Dove-feathered raven, wolvish-ravening lamb!
Was ever book containing such vile matter
So fairly bound? O! that deceit should dwell
In such a gorgeous palace.

Nurse: There's no trust,
No faith, no honesty in men. All perjured,
All forsworn, all naught, all dissemblers.
Shame come to Romeo!

Juliet: Blistered be thy tongue
For such a wish! He was not born to shame.
Upon his brow shame is ashamed to sit;
For 'tis a throne where honor may be crowned
Sole monarch of the universal earth.
O, what a beast was I to chide at him!

Literary terms

"Beautiful tyrant, fiend angelical! Dove-feathered raven, wolvish-ravening lamb!" are good examples of *oxymorons*.

Juliet can't believe that Romeo has killed Tybalt for he looks so trustworthy.

Nurse says that all men are liars and cannot be trusted.

Think about it

Juliet is confused. Would you be, if you were in her position?

Do you feel sorry for her?

There is a chance that Juliet and Romeo can meet for a last time.

Will you speak well of him that killed your cousin?

Shall I speak ill of him that is my husband?

My husband lives, that Tybalt would have slain, and Tybalt's dead that would have slain my husband.

Where is my father and my mother?

Weeping and wailing over Tybalt's corpse. Will you go to them?

Wash they his wounds with tears? Mine shall be spent when theirs are dry, for Romeo's banishment.

Come, Nurse, I'll to my wedding bed, and Death, not Romeo, take my maidenhead.

I'll find Romeo to comfort you. He is hid at Laurence' cell.

O find him and bid him come to take his last farewell.

Father, what news?

Not body's death but body's banishment.

Be merciful, say "death." There is no world without Verona walls.

O rude unthankfulness! The kind Prince, taking thy part, turned that black word death to banishment.

'Tis torture, and not mercy. Heaven is here where Juliet lives.

Let me dispute with thee of **thy estate**.

Thou canst not speak of that thou dost not feel.

Arise. One knocks. Good Romeo, hide thyself.

Who knocks so hard?

I come from Lady Juliet.

Literary terms

"Not body's death but body's banishment" is a good example of *alliteration*.

thy estate – your situation

| Act 3
Scene 3 | The Nurse finds Romeo in the same state that Juliet is in. Friar Laurence and the Nurse try to talk some sense into Romeo, because he is threatening to kill himself. They plan for him to visit Juliet and then go to Mantua. | |

Nurse: O holy friar, O, tell me, holy friar,
Where is my lady's lord? Where's Romeo?

Friar Laurence: There on the ground, with his own
tears made drunk.

Nurse: O! he is even in my mistress' case,
Just in her case! Piteous predicament! Even so lies she,
Blubbering and weeping, weeping and blubbering.
Stand up, stand up. Stand an you be a man.
For Juliet's sake, for her sake, rise and stand.

Romeo: Spakest thou of Juliet? How is it with her?
Doth not she think me an old murderer?
Where is she? And how doth she? And what says
My **concealed** lady to our cancelled love?

concealed – his secret wife

Nurse: O, she says nothing, sir, but weeps and weeps,
And now falls on her bed, and then starts up,
And Tybalt calls, and then on Romeo cries,
And then falls down again.

Romeo: As if that name,
Shot from the deadly level of a gun,
Did murder her, as that name's cursèd hand
Murdered her kinsman. O, tell me, friar, tell me,
In what vile part of this anatomy
Doth my name lodge? Tell me, that I may **sack**
The hateful mansion.

sack – attack and destroy

[*Romeo draws his sword*]

Friar Laurence: Hold thy desperate hand!
Art thou a man? Thy form cries out thou art.
Thy tears are womanish; thy wild acts denote
The unreasonable fury of a beast.
Thou hast amazed me. By my holy order,
I thought thy disposition better tempered.

Hast thou slain Tybalt? Wilt thou slay thyself,
And slay thy lady that in thy life lives,
By doing damnèd hate upon thyself?
What! rouse thee, man; thy Juliet is alive,
For whose dear sake thou wast but lately dead:
There art thou happy. Tybalt would kill thee,
But thou slewest Tybalt: there art thou happy.
The law that threatened death becomes thy friend
And turns it to exile: there art thou happy.
A pack of blessings light upon thy back;
Go, get thee to thy love, as was decreed.
Ascend her chamber, hence and comfort her.
But look thou stay not till the watch be set,
For then thou canst not pass to Mantua,
Where thou shalt live till we can find a time
To **blaze** your marriage, reconcile your friends,   **blaze** – to tell everyone
Beg pardon of the Prince, and call thee back.
Go before, Nurse. Commend me to thy lady;
And bid her hasten all the house to bed,
Which heavy sorrow makes them apt unto.
Romeo is coming.

Nurse: My lord, I'll tell my lady you will come.
Hie you, make haste, for it grows very late.

Friar Laurence: Either be gone before the **watch be set**   **watch be set** – guards are posted
Or by the break of day disguised from hence.
Sojourn in Mantua. I'll find out your man,   **Sojourn** – stay
And he shall signify from time to time
Every good hap to you that chances here.
Give me thy hand. 'Tis late. Farewell. Goodnight.

Think about it

Do you agree that Romeo is acting silly?

Should he pull himself together and think himself lucky?

Is Friar Laurence right to promise Romeo that one day he will be able to return and everything will turn out right?

Complications! Remember Paris? Juliet's father has agreed to let him marry Juliet!

These times of woe afford no times to woo.

Paris, I think she will be ruled in all respects by me. Nay, I doubt it not.

Wife, go you to her ere you go to bed...

... and bid her, mark you me, on Wednesday next – but, what day is this?

Monday, my lord.

Well, Wednesday is too soon. A Thursday tell her, she shall be married.

We'll have some half a dozen friends and there an end.

I would that Thursday were tomorrow.

Well, get you gone. A Thursday be it.

Prepare her, wife, against this wedding day.

| Act 3 Scene 5 | Romeo and Juliet have spent their wedding night together. Now they must part because he has to go to Mantua. Juliet's mother is coming! |

Juliet: Wilt thou be gone? It is not yet near day.
It was the nightingale and not the lark,
That pierced the fearful hollow of thine ear.

Romeo: It was the lark, the herald of the morn,
No nightingale. Look, love, what envious streaks
Do lace the severing clouds in yonder east.
Night's candles are burnt out, and jocund day
Stands tiptoe on the misty mountain tops.
I must be gone and live, or stay and die.

Juliet: Yond light is not daylight, I know it, I.
It is some meteor that the sun exhaled
To be to thee this night a torchbearer
And light thee on thy way to Mantua.
Therefore stay yet. Thou need'st not to be gone.

Romeo: Let me be ta'en; let me be put to death,
I am content, so thou wilt have it so.
I have more care to stay than will to go.
Come death, and welcome. Juliet wills it so.
How is't, my soul? Let's talk. It is not day.

Juliet: It is, it is. Hie hence, be gone, away!
It is the lark that sings so out of tune,
Straining harsh discords and unpleasing sharps.
Some say the lark makes sweet **division**.
This doth not so, for she divideth us.

[*The Nurse comes in*]

Nurse: Madam.

Juliet: Nurse?

Nurse: Your lady mother is coming to your chamber:
The day is broke; be wary; look about.

[*The Nurse leaves*]

> **Literary terms**
>
> "Night's candles are burnt out, and jocund day stands tiptoe on the misty mountain tops" is a good example of *personification*.

Romeo will risk death and stay, but Juliet realizes that he must go.

division – elaborate variations on a melody

Juliet: Then, window, let day in and let life out.

Romeo: Farewell, farewell. One kiss and I'll descend.
                    [*Romeo climbs down the rope ladder*]

Juliet: I must hear from thee every day in the hour,
For in a minute there are many days.
O, by this count I shall be much in years
Ere I again behold my Romeo.

Romeo: Farewell. I will omit no opportunity
That may convey my greetings, love, to thee.

Juliet: O think'st thou we shall ever meet again?

Romeo: I doubt it not; and all these woes shall serve
For sweet discourses in our times to come.

Juliet: O God, I have an ill-divining soul!
Methinks I see thee, now thou art so low,
As one dead in the bottom of a tomb.
Either my eyesight fails, or thou lookest pale.

Romeo: And trust me, love, in my eye so do you.
Dry sorrow drinks our blood. Adieu, adieu.

Think about it

Juliet says that Romeo looks "As one dead in the bottom of a tomb."

Does that give you a clue about what might happen?

Juliet finds out she has to marry Paris!

Why, how now Juliet?

Madam, I am not well.

Evermore weeping for your cousin's death? We will have vengeance for it, fear thou not.

I'll send to one in Mantua, shall give him such an unaccustomed **dram** that he shall soon keep Tybalt company.

I never shall be satisfied with Romeo, till I behold him – dead.

But now I'll tell thee joyful tidings, girl.

Thou hast a careful father, one who hath sorted out a sudden day of joy.

Early next Thursday morn, Paris, at Saint Peter's church shall happily make thee there a joyful bride.

I pray you, tell my lord and father I will not marry yet.

Here comes your father, tell him so yourself . . .

. . . and see how he will take it at your hands.

dram – a drink (of poison)

<table>
<tr><td>Act 3
Scene 5</td><td>Juliet's father is furious that she will not marry Paris. He says that he will have nothing to do with her and Lady Capulet says the same. Even the Nurse advises her to marry Paris. Juliet plans to go to Friar Laurence for advice. If nothing works she will kill herself.</td><td></td></tr>
</table>

Capulet: How now, wife? Have you delivered to her our decree?

Lady Capulet: Ay, sir, but she will none, she gives you thanks.
I would the fool were married to her grave.

Capulet: How, will she none? Doth she not give us thanks?
Is she not proud? Doth she not count her blessed,
Unworthy as she is, that we have wrought
So worthy a gentleman to be her bridegroom?

Juliet: Not proud you have, but thankful that you have.
Proud can I never be of what I hate,
But thankful even for hate that is meant love.

Capulet: But fettle your fine joints 'gainst Thursday next
To go with Paris to Saint Peter's church,
Or I will drag thee on a **hurdle** thither.

hurdle – a sled used to transport animals to be slaughtered

Juliet: Good father, I beseech you on my knees,
Hear me with patience but to speak a word.

Capulet: Hang thee, young baggage, disobedient wretch!
I tell thee what, get thee to church o' Thursday,
Or never after look me in the face.

Nurse: God in heaven bless her!
You are to blame, my lord, to rate her so.

Capulet: And why, my lady wisdom? Hold your tongue.
God's bread, it makes me mad.
My care hath been to have her matched. And having now provided
A gentleman of noble parentage,
And then to have a wretched **puling** fool.
To answer "I'll not wed. I cannot love.
I am too young. I pray you, pardon me."

puling – whining

An you be mine, I'll give you to my friend.
An you be not, hang, beg, starve, die in the streets,
For, by my soul, I'll ne'er acknowledge thee.

[*Capulet leaves*]

Juliet: O! sweet my mother, cast me not away.
Delay this marriage for a month, a week,
Or, if you do not, make the bridal bed
In that dim monument where Tybalt lies.

Lady Capulet: Talk not to me, for I'll not speak a word.
Do as thou wilt, for I have done with thee.

[*Lady Capulet leaves*]

Juliet: O God! O nurse, how shall this be prevented?
What sayst thou? Hast thou not a word of joy?

Nurse: Faith, here it is. Romeo is banished.
Then, since the case so stands as now it doth,
I think it best you married with the County.
O, he's a lovely gentleman!
Romeo's a **dishclout** to him. Beshrew my very heart,
I think you are happy in this second match,
For it excels your first.

dishclout – dishcloth

Juliet: Speakest thou from thy heart?

Nurse: And from my soul too.

Juliet: Well, thou hast comforted me marvelous much.
Go in and tell my lady I am gone,
Having displeased my father, to Laurence' cell
To make confession and to be absolved.

Nurse: Marry, I will; and this is wisely done. [*Nurse leaves*]

Juliet: Is it more sin to wish me thus forsworn,
Or to dispraise my lord with that same tongue
Which she hath praised him with above compare
So many thousand times?
I'll to the Friar to know his remedy.
If all else fail, myself have power to die.

> **Think about it**
>
> Can you spot another clue in the line "make the bridal bed in that dim monument where Tybalt lies"?
>
> Juliet is going to see Friar Laurence now. Remember his poisonous plants.
>
> What do you think of the Nurse's advice?

Paris thinks he really will marry Juliet. We know something different!

On Thursday, sir? The time is very short.

Capulet will have it so.

I like it not.

Here comes the lady.

Happily met, my lady and my wife.

That may be, sir, when I may be a wife.

That must be on Thursday next. 'Till then, adieu.

O shut the door and when thou hast done so, come weep with me: past hope, past cure, past help.

O Juliet, I already know thy grief.

Tell me not, Friar, that thou hearest of this, unless thou tell me how I may prevent it.

Be not so long to speak. I long to die if what thou speak'st speak not of remedy.

Act 4 Scene 1	Friar Laurence suggests a desperate plan. He tells Juliet to drink a liquid that will make her seem dead. She will sleep for 42 hours and wake up in the family tomb. He will write to Romeo and they will both wait for Juliet to wake.	

Friar Laurence: Hold, daughter, I do spy a kind of hope.
And, if thou darest, I'll give thee remedy.

Juliet: O, bid me leap, rather than marry Paris,
From off the battlements of any tower,
Or bid me go into a new-made grave
And hide me with a dead man in his shroud.

Friar Laurence: Hold, then. Go home; be merry; give consent
To marry Paris. Wednesday is tomorrow.
Tomorrow night look that thou lie alone.
Take thou this **vial**, being then in bed,
And this distilling liquor drink thou off;
When presently through all thy veins shall run
A cold and drowsy humor; for no pulse.
No warmth, no breath, shall testify thou livest.
And in this borrowed likeness of shrunk death
Thou shalt continue two and forty hours
And then awake as from a pleasant sleep.
Thou shalt be borne to that same ancient vault
Where all the kindred of the Capulets lie.
In the meantime, against thou shalt awake,
Shall Romeo by my letters know our drift,
And hither shall he come, and he and I
Will watch thy waking, and that very night
Shall Romeo bear thee hence to Mantua.

vial – small bottle

Juliet: Give me, give me! O, tell me not of fear.

Friar Laurence: Get you gone. Be strong in this resolve.
I'll send a friar with speed to Mantua
With letters to thy lord.

Think about it

How would you describe Juliet in this scene?

Can you see how anything might go wrong with this plan?

How now my headstrong! Where have you been gadding?

Where I have learned me to repent the sin of disobedient opposition. Henceforward I am ever ruled by you.

I'll have this knot knit up tomorrow morning.

Not till Thursday. There is time enough.

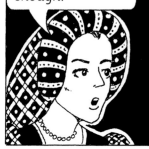

We'll go to church tomorrow.

Go thou to Juliet, help to deck her up. I will to Paris to prepare him against tomorrow.

Need you my help?

No, madam. So please you let me now be left alone.

Get thee to bed and rest, for thou hast need.

Act 4 Scene 3	Juliet is alone. She is worried in case the drink is poison and she will die. She is scared that if she wakes up early in the tomb, she will suffocate or go mad.	

Juliet: Farewell. God knows when we shall meet again.
Come vial.
What if this mixture do not work at all?
Shall I be married then tomorrow morning?
No, No, this shall forbid it. Lie thou there.

[*Juliet places a dagger by her bed*]

What if it be a poison which the friar
Subtly hath ministered to have me dead,
Lest in this marriage he should be dishonored
Because he married me before to Romeo?
I will not entertain so bad a thought.
How if, when I am laid into the tomb,
I wake before the time that Romeo
Come to redeem me? There's a fearful point!
Shall I not then be stifled in the vault,
To whose foul mouth no healthsome air breathes in,
And there die strangled ere my Romeo comes?
Alack, alack, is it not like that I,
So early waking, what with loathsome smells
And shrieks like **mandrakes** torn out of the earth,
That living mortals, hearing them, run mad –
O, if I wake, shall I not be distraught,
Environèd with all these hideous fears,
And madly play with my forefathers' joints,
And pluck the mangled Tybalt from his shroud?
O look, methinks I see my cousin's ghost
Seeking out Romeo that did spit his body
Upon a rapier's point! Stay, Tybalt, stay!
Romeo, Romeo, Romeo! Here's drink. I drink to thee.

> **Literary terms**
>
> Juliet's speech is a *soliloquy.*

mandrakes – plants that were supposed to scream if they were dug up

> **Think about it**
>
> If you were Juliet, what would you be worried about right now?

Early next morning, Juliet is found dead. Only Friar Laurence and we know she is alive really.

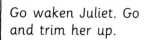

Go waken Juliet. Go and trim her up.

Help, help! My lady's dead!

Bring Juliet forth. Her lord is come.

She's dead!

Is the bride ready to go to church?

Ready to go, but never to return.

Have I thought long to see this morning's face, and doth it give me such a sight as this?

Everyone prepare to follow this fair corse unto her grave.

All things that we ordained festival, turn to black funeral.

Act 5 Scene 1	Romeo's servant tells him he has seen Juliet's funeral. He has no letters from the Friar. Romeo plans to buy poison and kill himself while he lies by Juliet in the tomb.

Romeo: My dreams presage some joyful news at hand.
I dreamt my lady came and found me dead
And breathed such life with kisses in my lips
That I revived and was an emperor. *[Enter Balthasar]*
News from Verona! How now, Balthasar?
Dost thou not bring me letters from the Friar?
How doth my lady? Is my father well?
How doth my Juliet? That I ask again,
For nothing can be ill if she be well.

Balthasar: Her body sleeps in Capel's monument.
I saw her laid low in her kindred's vault.

She is dead and in the tomb.

Romeo: Is it e'en so? Then I defy you, stars!
Thou knowest my lodging. Get me ink and paper,
And hire posthorses. I will hence tonight.

Balthasar: I do beseech you, sir, have patience.

Romeo: Leave me, and do the thing I bid thee do.
Hast thou no letters to me from the Friar?

Balthasar: No, my good lord.

Romeo: No matter, get thee gone,
And hire those horses: I'll be with thee straight.
  [Balthasar leaves]
Well, Juliet, I will lie with thee tonight.
I do remember an **apothecary**, and hereabouts he dwells.
To myself I said, an if a man did need a poison now,
Here lives a **caitiff** wretch would sell it him.

Think about it

"I dreamt my lady came and found me dead." What does that tell you might happen?

"Get me ink and paper." What do you think Romeo is going to do now?

apothecary – chemist

caitiff – miserable

Oh no! Romeo didn't get the letter telling him about the plan! Friar John, who was supposed to deliver it, explains what happened to Friar Laurence.

Welcome from Mantua. What says Romeo?

Going to find a brother out to **associate** me, the searchers of the town, suspecting that we both were in a house where the infectious **pestilence** did reign, would not let us go forth.

Who bore my letter then to Romeo?

I could not send it — here it is again.

Unhappy fortune. The letter was of dear import ...

... and the neglecting it may do much danger.

Now must I to the monument alone. Within three hours will Juliet awake. But I will write again to Mantua, and keep her at my cell till Romeo come.

associate – accompany   **pestilence** – plague

Act 5 Scene 3	Paris and his page (servant) are at the tomb. Romeo arrives and fights and kills Paris. Romeo breaks into the tomb, sees what he thinks is Juliet's corpse and poisons himself.	

Romeo: Give me that **mattock** and the wrenching iron.
Hold, take this letter. Early in the morning
See thou deliver it to my lord and father.
Give me the light and do not interrupt me in my course.
Why I descend into this bed of death
Is partly to behold my lady's face
But chiefly to take thence from her dead finger
A precious ring, a ring that I must use
In dear employment. Therefore hence, be gone.

mattock – a tool like a pickaxe

Balthasar: I will be gone, sir, and not trouble you.

Romeo: So shalt thou show me friendship.
Live, and be prosperous, and farewell, good fellow.

Balthasar: For all this same, I'll hide me hereabout.
His looks I fear, and his intents I doubt.   [*Balthasar hides*]

Romeo: Thou detestable **maw**, thou womb of death
Gorged with the dearest morsel of the earth,
Thus I enforce thy rotten jaws to open,
And in despite I'll cram thee with more **food**.

maw – stomach

Romeo will be the "food."

Paris: This is that haughty Montague
That murdered my love's cousin – with which grief
It is supposed the fair creature died.   [*Paris steps forward*]
Stop thy unhallowed toil, vile Montague.
Can vengeance be pursued further than death?
Condemnèd villain, I do apprehend thee.
Obey and go with me, for thou must die.

Romeo: I must indeed, and therefore came I hither.
Stay not, be gone, live, and hereafter say
A mad man's mercy bid thee run away.

Page: O Lord, they fight! I will go call the **Watch**.

watch – the city guard

Paris: O I am slain! If thou be merciful,
Open the tomb, lay me with Juliet.   *[Paris dies]*

Romeo: In faith I will. Let me peruse this face.
Mercutio's kinsman, noble County Paris!
What said my man as we rode? I think
He told me Paris should have married Juliet.
Said he not so? Or did I dream it so?
Death, lie thou there, by a dead man interred.
                         [He lays Paris in the tomb]
O my love, my wife,
Death that hath sucked the honey of thy breath,
Hath had no power yet upon thy beauty.
Thou art not conquered. Beauty's **ensign** yet
Is crimson in thy lips and in thy cheeks,
And Death's pale flag is not advanced there.
Why art thou yet so fair? I still will stay with thee
And never from this palace of dim night
Depart again. Here, here will I remain
With worms that are thy chambermaids.
Eyes, look your last. Arms, take your last embrace!
And lips seal with a righteous kiss
A dateless bargain to engrossing Death.
Here's to my love!   *[He drinks the poison]*
O true apothecary, thy drugs are quick.
Thus with a kiss I die.

> **Literary terms**
>
> This speech by Romeo is a *soliloquy*.

ensign – military flag or banner

Think about it

What does Paris think Romeo is going to do in the tomb?

Read again "Death that hath sucked the honey of thy breath
          Hath had no power yet upon thy beauty:
          Thou art not conquered. Beauty's ensign yet
          Is crimson in thy lips and in thy cheeks."

What has Romeo not realized?

| **Act 5 Scene 3** | Friar Laurence arrives at the tomb. He meets Balthasar, Romeo's servant, and begins to realize that the plan has gone dreadfully wrong. |

Who's there? A friend.

Tell me, what torch burneth in the Capel's monument? Who is it?

Romeo.

Go with me to the vault.

I dare not, sir.

Stay then, I'll go alone.

Fear comes upon me. O, much I fear some ill **unthrifty** thing.

As I did sleep, I dreamt my master and another fought, and that my master slew him.

What blood is this? What mean these masterless and gory swords to lie discolored by this place of peace?

unthrifty – evil

<table>
<tr>
<td>Act 5
Scene 3</td>
<td>Juliet wakes up only to be told by the Friar that Romeo and Paris are dead. She sees Romeo and will not leave him. The Friar goes and Juliet kills herself.</td>
</tr>
</table>

Friar Laurence: Romeo! O, pale! Who else? What, Paris too?
And steeped in blood? Ah what an unkind hour
Is guilty of this lamentable chance?
The lady stirs.

[Juliet wakes up]

Juliet: O comfortable Friar, where is my lord?
I do remember well where I should be,
And there I am. Where is my Romeo?

Friar Laurence: I hear some noise. Lady, come from that nest
Of death, contagion, and unnatural sleep.
**A greater power than we can contradict
Hath thwarted our intents**. Come, come away.
Thy husband in thy bosom there lies dead,
And Paris too. Come, I'll dispose of thee
Among a sisterhood of holy nuns.
Stay not to question for the Watch is coming.
Come, go, good Juliet. I dare no longer stay.

> Something beyond our control has spoiled our plans.

Juliet: Go, get thee hence, for I will not away.

[Friar Laurence leaves]

What's here? A cup closed in my true love's hand?
Poison, I see, hath been his timeless end.
O **churl**, drunk all, and left no friendly drop
To help me after? I will kiss thy lips.
Haply some poison yet doth hang on them
To make me die with a restorative.   *[Juliet kisses Romeo]*
Thy lips are warm!

> **churl** – selfish one

Watchman: [*Outside the tomb*] Lead, boy. Which way?

Juliet: Yea, noise? Then I'll be brief. O happy dagger.
This is thy sheath. There rust, and let me die.

[Juliet stabs herself and dies]

> **Think about it**
>
> Why is Friar Laurence impatient to get away?
>
> What do you think of Juliet's reactions?

The three young people are found dead.

This is the place.

Here lies the County slain and Juliet bleeding, warm and newly dead.

Go tell the Prince. Run to the Capulets. Raise up the Montagues.

What misadventure is so early up?

What should it be, that is so shrieked abroad?

The people in the streets cry "Romeo," some "Juliet," others "Paris."

Here lies the County Paris slain, and Romeo dead, and Juliet, dead before, warm, and new killed.

Search, seek, and know how this foul murder comes.

Here is a friar, and Romeo's man, with instruments upon them fit to open these dead men's tombs.

Act 5 Scene 3	Friar Laurence tells the Prince the story as he knows it. Romeo's letter to his father confirms what the Friar has said.	

Prince: Come Montague: for thou art early up
To see thy son and heir more early down.

Montague: Alas my liege, my wife is dead tonight;
Grief of my son's exile hath stopped her breath.
What further woe conspires against my age?

Prince: Look, and thou shalt see.
Bring forth the parties of suspicion.

Friar Laurence: I am the greatest, able to do least,
Yet most suspected, as the time and place
Doth make against me, of this direful murder.

Prince: Then say at once what thou dost know in this.

Friar Laurence: I will be brief.
Romeo, there dead, was husband to that Juliet,
And she, there dead, that Romeo's faithful wife.
I married them, and their stol'n marriage day
Was Tybalt's doomsday, whose untimely death
Banished the new-made bridegroom from this city,
For whom, and not for Tybalt, Juliet pined.
You, to remove that siege of grief from her,
Betrothed and would have married her perforce
To County Paris. Then comes she to me,
And with wild looks bid me devise some mean
To rid her from this second marriage,
Or in my cell there would she kill herself.
Then gave I her – so tutored by my art –
A sleeping potion, which so took effect
As I intended, for it wrought on her
The form of death. Meantime I writ to Romeo
That he should hither come as this dire night
To help to take her from her borrowed grave,

56

Being the time the potion's force should cease.
But he which bore my letter, Friar John,
Was stayed by accident, and yesternight
Returned my letter back. Then all alone
At the prefixèd hour of her waking
Came I to take her from her kindred's vault,
Meaning to keep her closely at my cell
Till I conveniently could send to Romeo.
But when I came, some minute ere the time
Of her awakening, here untimely lay
The noble Paris and true Romeo dead.
She wakes, and I entreated her come forth
And bear this work of heaven with patience.
But then a noise did scare me from the tomb,
And she, too desperate, would not go with me
But, as it seems, did violence on herself.
All this I know, and to the marriage
Her Nurse is privy; and if aught in this   He tells them that the Nurse knew
Miscarried by my fault, let my old life   about Romeo and Juliet's marriage.
Be sacrificed some hour before his time
Unto the rigor of severest law.

Prince: We still have known thee for a holy man.
Where's Romeo's man? What can he say to this?

Balthasar: I brought my master news of Juliet's death,
And then **in post** he came from Mantua   **in post** – quickly
To this same place, to this same monument.
This letter he early bid me give his father.

Prince: Give me the letter, I will look on it.
This letter doth make good the Friar's words,
Their course of love, the tidings of her death;
And here he writes that he did buy a poison
Of a poo 'pothecary, and therewithal
Came to this vault to die and lie with Juliet.

Think about it

Why do we have to hear the whole story again from the Friar?

The two families make the peace. Statues in gold of Romeo and Juliet will be placed in Verona.

Where be these enemies? Capulet, Montague. See what a scourge is laid upon your hate.

And I have lost **a brace** of kinsmen. All are punished.

O brother Montague, give me thy hand.

I will raise her statue in pure gold. That while Verona by that name is known, There shall be no figure at such rate be set As that of true and faithful Juliet.

As rich shall Romeo's by his lady's lie, Poor sacrifices of our **emnity**.

A glooming peace this morning with it brings. The sun for sorrow will not show his head. Go hence to have more talk of these sad things. Some shall be pardoned and some punished. For never was a story of more woe Than this of Juliet and her Romeo.

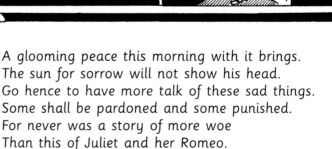

THE END

a brace – two (Mercutio and Paris)
emnity – hatred

Literary terms

"glooming peace" is a good example of an *oxymoron*.

PICTURE THIS!
Shakespeare

William Shakespeare's
Romeo and Juliet

The bodies of two young lovers
lie in a cold tomb.
One has been stabbed
and the other poisoned.
It is less than a week
since they first met . . .

Picture This! Shakespeare **Titles**
Currently Available from Barron's:
Macbeth • A Midsummer Night's Dream
Romeo and Juliet • Twelfth Night

ISBN-13: 978-0-7641-3144-8
ISBN-10: 0-7641-3144-3

11 02
CLEARANCE
$ 399

50899>

9 780764 13 48

$8.99   Canada $10.99
www.barronseduc.com

BARRON'S